AF559559

Vaishno Devi Chalisa

Vaishno Devi Chalisa

Published in Sanskriti Press
Rupa Publications India Pvt. Ltd 2025
161-B/4, Gulmohar House,
Yusuf Sarai Community Centre,
New Delhi 110049

Sales centres:
Bengaluru Chennai
Hyderabad Kolkata Mumbai

P-ISBN: 978-93-7003-779-3
E-ISBN: 978-93-7003-415-0

First impression 2025

10 9 8 7 6 5 4 3 2 1

Printed in India

Contents

Introduction / 7

Chalisa / 11

माँ वैष्णों देवी की आरती / 56

Maa Vaishno Devi Aarti / 58

Introduction

Maa Vaishno Devi Chalisa is a powerful and deeply devotional hymn composed in honour of **Maa Vaishno Devi**, one of the most revered and beloved manifestations of the Divine Mother in Hinduism. Nestled in the Trikuta Mountains of Jammu and Kashmir, the holy shrine of Vaishno Devi draws millions of devotees every year, who undertake the sacred pilgrimage to seek her blessings, protection, and grace. The Chalisa serves as both a poetic offering and a spiritual pathway, invoking her divine presence in the heart of the devotee.

Maa Vaishno Devi is believed to be the combined embodiment of the three great goddesses: **Maa Kali, Maa Lakshmi** and **Maa**

Saraswati, representing strength, wealth and wisdom respectively. As the protector of dharma and the destroyer of evil, she incarnated on Earth to uphold righteousness and to bless humanity with her divine energy. Her story, rich with mystical events and spiritual significance, forms the core of the Chalisa, which beautifully recounts her descent, her penance, her divine acts, and her eternal abode in the holy cave of Trikuta.

The **Chalisa**, composed in forty verses (chaupais) with introductory and concluding dohas (couplets), praises Maa Vaishno Devi's many forms and leelas (divine acts). It narrates her birth, her penance to please Lord Rama, her transformation through the ages, her encounter with Bhairon Nath, and her eternal establishment in the sacred cave. It also describes the celestial beings who guard her, the divine cave where she resides, the rituals of worship offered by devotees, and the unwavering faith that draws her bhaktas (devotees) to her door.

Each verse of the Chalisa is filled with deep spiritual emotion and surrender. It is believed that regular recitation of the Maa Vaishno Devi Chalisa brings about peace of mind, fulfillment of desires, removal of obstacles, and divine protection. It strengthens one's faith and connects the soul with the nurturing and powerful presence of the Mother. For those facing hardship, spiritual uncertainty, or emotional distress, this Chalisa acts as a source of divine reassurance and strength.

In the **Kaliyug**, the current age of turmoil and spiritual decline, the significance of Maa Vaishno Devi's worship has only grown. She is considered the ever-awake goddess—a **Jagat Janani**, the Mother of the Universe, who listens to every sincere prayer and rushes to the aid of her children. Whether one visits her shrine in person or calls out to her from afar, her presence is immediate, and her grace, unconditional.

Reciting this Chalisa is more than an act of devotion—it is a spiritual journey. With each line, the devotee steps closer to the divine cave of the heart, where Maa Vaishno resides eternally. Her energy, her story, and her love flow through these verses like a sacred river, bathing the soul in light and truth.

Chalisa

॥ दोहा ॥

गरुड़ वाहिनी वैष्णवी
त्रिकुटा पर्वत धाम
काली, लक्ष्मी, सरस्वती,
शक्ति तुम्हें प्रणाम।

॥ **Doha** ॥

Garud vaahini Vaishnavi,
Trikuta parvat dhaam,
Kaali, Lakshmi, Saraswati,
Shakti tumhein pranaam.

Invocation Chaupai

O Vaishnavi, who rides the celestial eagle Garuda,
Your abode is on the sacred Trikuta mountain.
You embody Kali, Lakshmi, and Saraswati—
To you, O Divine Mother, I offer my salutations.

॥ चौपाई ॥

नमोः नमोः वैष्णो वरदानी,
कलि काल मे शुभ कल्याणी।
मणि पर्वत पर ज्योति तुम्हारी,
पिंडी रूप में हो अवतारी ॥

Namo namo Vaishno varadaani,
Kali kaal mein shubh kalyaani.
Mani parvat par jyoti tumhaari,
Pindi roop mein ho avataari.

Salutations again and again to Vaishno, the granter of boons,
O auspicious one, who brings welfare even in this dark age of Kali.
Your divine light shines upon the Mani Parvat,
And you manifest there in the form of a sacred pindi (divine rock form).

देवी देवता अंश दियो है,
रत्नाकर घर जन्म लियो है।
करी तपस्या राम को पाऊं,
त्रेता की शक्ति कहलाऊं ।।

Devi devata ansh diyo hai,
Ratnaakar ghar janm liyo hai.
Kari tapasya Ram ko paaun,
Treta ki shakti kehlaaun.

You carry the divine essence of all gods
and goddesses,
And were born in the home of the ocean
(symbolic of purity and power).
You performed deep pcnancc to attain
Lord Ram,
Thus becoming known as the divine
Shakti of the Treta Yuga.

कहा राम मणि पर्वत जाओ,
कलियुग की देवी कहलाओ।
विष्णु रूप से कल्कि बनकर,
लूंगा शक्ति रूप बदलकर ॥

Kaha Ram: "Mani parvat jaao,
Kaliyug ki devi kehlaao.
Vishnu roop se Kalki bankar,
Loonga shakti roop badalkar."

Lord Ram instructed: "Go to the Mani Parvat,
In Kaliyug, you shall be worshipped as the great Goddess.
When I return in my Kalki form at the end of the age,
I will reclaim your Shakti and bring transformation."

तब तक त्रिकुटा घाटी जाओ,
गुफा अंधेरी जाकर पाओ।
काली-लक्ष्मी-सरस्वती मां,
करेंगी पोषण पार्वती मां ॥

Tab tak Trikuta ghaati jaao,
Gufa andheri jaakar paao.
Kaali-Lakshmi-Saraswati maa,
Karengee poshan Parvati maa.

Until then, go dwell in the valleys of Trikuta,
Find the hidden cave and meditate in the dark.
With you shall be Mother Kali, Lakshmi, and Saraswati,
And Mother Parvati will nurture you.

ब्रह्मा, विष्णु, शंकर द्वारे,
हनुमत, भैरों प्रहरी प्यारे।
रिद्धि, सिद्धि चंवर डुलावें,
कलियुग-वासी पूजत आवें ।।

Brahma, Vishnu, Shankar dwaare,
Hanumat, Bhairav prahari pyaare.
Riddhi, Siddhi chamvar dulaaven,
Kaliyug-vaasi poojat aaven.

Brahma, Vishnu, and Shiva guard your doorway,
Alongside Hanuman and Bhairav, your beloved sentinels.
Riddhi and Siddhi fan you with chauris (divine whisks),
And people of Kaliyug come to offer you worship.

पान सुपारी ध्वजा नारीयल,
चरणामृत चरणों का निर्मल।
दिया फलित वर माँ मुस्काई,
करन तपस्या पर्वत आई ॥

Paan supaari dhwaja naariyal,
Charanamrit charanon ka nirmal.
Diya phalit var maa muskaayi,
Karan tapasya parvat aayi.

With betel leaves, coconuts, flags, and pure offerings,
They bring sanctified water from your lotus feet.
You smile upon their devotion and grant their wishes,
Then return to your mountain to continue your meditation.

कलि काल की भड़की ज्वाला,
इक दिन अपना रूप निकाला।
कन्या बन नगरोटा आई,
योगी भैरों दिया दिखाई ।।

Kali kaal ki bhadki jwaala,
Ek din apna roop nikaala.
Kanya ban Nagrota aayi,
Yogi Bhairav diya dikhaayi.

In the age of Kali, when evil flames flared high,
You revealed your true form.
Taking the guise of a young maiden, you came to Nagrota,
Where the yogi Bhairav caught sight of you.

रूप देख सुंदर ललचाया,
पीछे-पीछे भागा आया।
कन्याओं के साथ मिली माँ,
कौल-कंदौली तभी चली माँ ।।

Roop dekh sundar lalchaaya,
Peechhe-peechhe bhaaga aaya.
Kanyaon ke saath mili maa,
Kaul-Kandauli tabhi chali maa.

Mesmerized by your divine beauty,
He was filled with desire and followed you.
As you joined a group of girls,
You journeyed onward to the village of Kandauli.

देवा माई दर्शन दीना,
पवन रूप हो गई प्रवीणा।
नवरात्रों में लीला रचाई,
भक्त श्रीधर के घर आई ।।

Deva maai darshan deena,
Pavan roop ho gayi praveena.
Navratron mein leela rachaayi,
Bhakt Shridhar ke ghar aayi.

There, you revealed your divine form to Bhairav,
And became one with the wind to escape his gaze.
During Navratri, you performed divine leelas (playful acts),
And visited the home of your devotee, Shri Dhar.

योगिन को भण्डारा दीनी,
सबने रूचिकर भोजन कीना।
मांस, मदिरा भैरों मांगी,
रूप पवन कर इच्छा त्यागी ।।

Yogin ko bhandara deeni,
Sabne ruchikar bhojan keeni.
Maans, madira Bhairav maangi,
Roop pavan kar ichchha tyaagi.

You blessed the yoginis with a grand feast,
And all joyfully partook in the sacred meal.
Bhairav demanded meat and wine,
But you, pure as the wind, renounced such desires.

बाण मारकर गंगा निकली,
पर्वत भागी हो मतवाली।
चरण रखे आ एक शीला जब,
चरण-पादुका नाम पड़ा तब ।।

Baan maarkar Ganga nikli,
Parvat bhaagi ho matwaali.
Charan rakhe aa ek sheela jab,
Charan-paaduka naam pada tab.

You struck an arrow into the earth and
the Ganga sprang forth,
As the mountain trembled and fled.
You placed your feet upon a stone slab,
Which then came to be known as "Charan
Paduka"—the mark of your feet.

पीछे भैरों था बलकारी,
चोटी गुफा में जाय पधारी।
नौ मह तक किया निवासा,
चली फोड़कर किया प्रकाशा ॥

Peechhe Bhairav tha balkari,
Choti gufa mein jaay padhaari.
Nau mah tak kiya nivaasa,
Chali phodkar kiya prakaasha.

Bhairav, still pursuing you,
Followed you into the cave on the mountain peak.
You dwelled there in silence for nine months,
And then burst forth with radiant light.

आद्या शक्ति-ब्रह्म कुमारी,
कहलाई माँ आद कुंवारी।
गुफा द्वार पहुँची मुस्काई,
लांगुर वीर ने आज्ञा पाई ।।

Aadya shakti-Brahma kumaari,
Kehlaayi maa Aad Kunwaari.
Gufa dwar pahunchi muskaayi,
Langur veer ne aagya paayi.

You are the primordial Shakti, the Brahma Kumari,
Forever known as the original virgin goddess.
You reached the cave's entrance with a smile,
And Langoor Veer (monkey warrior) received your command.

भागा-भागा भैंरो आया,
रक्षा हित निज शस्त्र चलाया।
पड़ा शीश जा पर्वत ऊपर,
किया क्षमा जा दिया उसे वर ।।

Bhaaga-bhaaga Bhairav aaya,
Raksha hit nij shastr chalaaya.
Pada sheesh jaa parvat oopar,
Kiya kshama jaa diya use var.

Bhairav arrived, determined to fight,
But you, for protection, drew your divine weapon.
You severed his head, which flew to the mountain top,
Yet forgave him and granted him a boon.

अपने संग में पुजवाऊंगी,
भैंरो घाटी बनवाऊंगी।
पहले मेरा दर्शन होगा,
पीछे तेरा सुमिरन होगा ।।

Apne sang mein pujvaaoongi,
Bhairav ghaati banvaaoongi.
Pehle mera darshan hoga,
Peechhe tera sumiran hoga.

You declared, "You too shall be
worshipped along with me,
And a sacred Bhairav Valley shall be
established for you.
My darshan (vision) will always come
first,
But after that, you will be remembered."

बैठ गई मां पिंडी होकर,
चरणों में बहता जल झर झर ।
चौंसठ योगिनी-भैंरो पर्वत,
सप्तऋषि आ करते सुमिरन ॥

Baith gayi maa pindi hokar,
Charanon mein bahta jal jhar-jhar.
Chaunsath yogini-Bhairav parvat,
Saptarishi aa karte sumiran.

Then you sat in the form of a pindi
(divine stone),
While sacred water flowed in streams at
your feet.
Sixty-four yoginis and Bhairav reside in
the mountain,
And even the seven great sages come to
remember you.

घंटा ध्वनि पर्वत पर बाजे,
गुफा निराली सुंदर लागे।
भक्त श्रीधर पूजन कीन,
भक्ति सेवा का वर लीन ॥

Ghanta dhwani parvat par baaje,
Gufa niraali sundar laage.
Bhakt Shridhar poojan keena,
Bhakti seva ka var leena.

Bells resound across the holy peak,
And the cave radiates divine beauty.
Your devotee Shri Dhar offered his worship,
And earned your blessings through service and love.

सेवक ध्यानूं तुमको ध्याना,
ध्वजा व चोला आन चढ़ाया।
सिंह सदा दर पहरा देता,
पंजा शेर का दुःख हर लेता ॥

Sevak Dhyanun tumko dhyaana,
Dhwaja va chola aan chadhaaya.
Singh sada dar pahra deta,
Panja sher ka dukh har leta.

Your true devotee meditates upon you
with deep devotion,
Bringing silken robes and fluttering flags.
The lion always guards your entrance,
And the paw of the lion removes all
suffering.

जम्बू द्वीप महाराज मनाया,
सर सोने का छत्र चढ़ाया ।
हीरे की मूरत संग प्यारी,
जगे अखण्ड इक जोत तुम्हारी ।।

Jambu dweep Maharaj manaaya,
Sar sone ka chhatra chadhaaya.
Heere ki moorat sang pyaari,
Jage akhand ik jyot tumhaari.

In the land of Jambu, a great king built
your temple,
And offered a golden umbrella at your
shrine.
With a jewel-studded image and heartfelt
love,
He established an eternal, ever-burning
flame of your presence.

आश्विन चौत्र नवरात्रे आऊं,
पिण्डी रानी दर्शन पाऊं।
सेवक' कमल' शरण तिहारी,
हरो वैष्णो विपत हमारी ।।

Ashwin Chaitra Navratre aaun,
Pindi Rani darshan paaun.
Sevak 'Kamal' sharan tihaari,
Haro Vaishno vipat hamaari.

I come during the Navratri of Ashwin and Chaitra,
To receive your darshan, O Queen of the Pindis.
Your humble servant 'Kamal' seeks your shelter—
O Vaishno Mata, please remove all my hardships.

॥ दोहा ॥

कलियुग में महिमा तेरी,
है माँ अपरंपार
धर्म की हानि हो रही,
प्रगट हो अवतार

॥ इति श्री वैष्णो देवी चालीसा ॥

Doha

Kaliyug mein mahima teri,
Hai maa aparampaar.
Dharm ki haani ho rahi,
Pragat ho avataar.

Iti Shri Vaishno Devi Chalisa

Doha

Your glory in the age of Kali is boundless,
O Mother—
Beyond the limits of thought or praise.
As righteousness declines in this world,
Please manifest once more in divine form.

Thus ends the Shri Vaishno Devi Chalisa

माँ वैष्णों देवी आरती

जय वैष्णवी माता, मैया जय वैष्णवी माता ।
हाथ जोड़ तेरे आगे, आरती मैं गाता ।।

शीश पे छत्र विराजे, मूरतिया प्यारी ।
गंगा बहती चरनन, ज्योति जगे न्यारी ।।

ब्रह्मा वेद पढ़े नित द्वारे, शंकर ध्यान धरे ।
सेवक चंवर डुलावत, नारद नृत्य करे ।।

सुन्दर गुफा तुम्हारी, मन को अति भावे ।
बार-बार देखन को, ऐ माँ मन चावे ।।

भवन पे झण्डे झूलें, घंटा ध्वनि बाजे ।
ऊँचा पर्वत तेरा, माता प्रिय लागे ।।

पान सुपारी ध्वजा नारियल, भेंट पुष्प मेवा ।
दास खड़े चरणों में, दर्शन दो देवा ।।

जो जन निश्चय करके, द्वार तेरे आवे ।
उसकी इच्छा पूरण, माता हो जावे ।।

इतनी स्तुति निश-दिन, जो नर भी गावे ।
कहते सेवक ध्यानू, सुख सम्पत्ति पावे ।।

Maa Vaishno Devi Aarti

Jai Vashnavi Mata,
Maiya Jai Vashnavi Mata ।
Hath Jod Tere Aage,
Aarti Mai Gaataa ॥

Sheesh Par Chatra Birajay,
Murtiyan Pyaari ।
Ganga Bahti Charnan,
Jyoti Jage Nyaari ॥

Brahma Ved Padhe Nit Dvare,
Shankar Dhyan Dhare ।
Sevat Chanvar Dulavat,
Narad Nritya Kare ॥

Sundar Gufa Tumhari,
Mann ko Ati Bhave ।
Baar-Baar Dekhn ko,
Ae Maa Mann Chave ॥

Bhawan Pe Jhande Jhulay,
Ghanta Dhwani Baajay ।
Uncha Parvat Tera,
Mata Priya Laagay ॥

Paan Supari Dhwaja nariyal,
Bhent Pushp Mewa ।
Dass Khadde Charnon mai,
Darshan Do Deva ॥

Jo Jan Nischay karke,
Dwar Tere Aavay ।
Uski Ichchha Puran
Mata Ho Jave ॥

Itani Stuti Nishdin,
Jo Nar Bhi Gave ।

Kahte Sevak Dhyanu,
Sukh Sampati Pave ॥

Maa Vaishno Devi Aarti

Victory to You, Vaishnavi Mata,
O Mother, Victory to You,
Vaishnavi Mata!
With folded hands I stand before You,
singing Your sacred Aarti.

A royal canopy rests upon Your head,
and Your idols are beautifully adorned,
The sacred Ganga flows at Your feet, and
a unique divine flame shines continuously.

At Your door, Brahma recites
the Vedas daily, and Lord
Shankar meditates upon You,

Devotees serve You, waving divine fans, while Sage Narad dances in Your praise.

Your sacred cave is so enchanting, it
deeply pleases the heart and mind,
Again and again, O Mother, the soul
longs to behold Your divine form.

Flags flutter proudly atop Your temple,
and the sound of bells echoes all around,
Your sacred mountain stands tall and
high—a place most dear to You,
O Mother.

Betel leaves, areca nuts, flags,
coconuts, and offerings of flowers
and sweets are brought,
This humble devotee stands at

Your feet—O Divine Mother,
please grant me Your darshan.

Whoever comes to Your door
with firm faith and devotion,
You fulfill all their wishes, O Mother—
they are never turned away.

Whoever sings Your praises daily
with love and devotion,
Says Your servant Dhyanū: that soul
attains happiness and prosperity.